While much petrol was distributed in cans by rail in the early years of motoring, this postcard from c.1905 shows the alternative. Companies that had been distributing lamp oil already had horse-drawn tankers in operation. Here an Anglo American Oil tanker is delivering Pratts Spirit in two-gallon cans as well as White Rose lamp oil to a cycle and motor accessory business.

Petroleum Collectables

Mike Berry

in association with the Michael Sedgwick Trust

Published by Shire Publications Ltd,
Midland House, West Way, Botley, Oxford OX2 0PH, UK.
(Website: www.shirebooks.co.uk)
Copyright © 2004 by Mike Berry.
First published 2004.
Transferred to digital print on demand 2011.
Shire Library 430. ISBN 978 0 74780 595 3.
Mike Berry is hereby identified as the author of this work
in accordance with Section 77 of the Copyright, Designs
and Patents Act 1988.

British Library Cataloguing in Publication Data:
Berry, Mike.
Petroleum collectables. – (Shire album; 430)
1. Service stations – Collectibles
2. Petroleum industry and trade – Collectibles
I. Title II. Michael Sedgwick Trust
629.2'86'075
ISBN-10 0 7478 0595 4.
ISBN-13 978 0 74780 595 3.

This work is published with the assistance of the Michael Sedgwick Trust. Founded in memory of the
famous motoring researcher and author Michael Sedgwick (1926–83), the Trust is a Registered Charity
to encourage the publishing of new research and recording of motoring history. Suggestions for future
projects or donations should be sent to the Hon. Sec. of the Michael Sedgwick Trust, c/o the National
Motor Museum, Beaulieu, Hampshire SO42 7ZN, England. For further details see the website:
www.sedgwicktrust.com

Cover: *Collection of vintage 1920s petrol cans on display at the Smallholders Show, Ardingly, West
Sussex, presented by Brian Blackman. (Photograph courtesy of Chris Parfitt)*

I would like to express my appreciation to Michael Ware, without whose help this book would not
have been possible. We have spent much time together preparing the content, during which he has
made copious notes from my ramblings and scripted them together to make a readable history of the
selling of petrol before the Second World War, and of the present-day interest in collecting the
artefacts from those years. I would also like to thank my wife, Jackie, who not only has supported my
unending quest for additions to my own collection, but has become obsessed herself! A thesis
researched by Trevor Lord on petrol stations and lodged at the National Motor Museum provided
very useful background information. Other help came from Nick Baldwin, Michael Worthington-
Williams, Malcolm Jeal, Andy Lane, Michael Tambini, Doug Hill, Robin Barnard, Mike and Sue
Richardson, Alan Baker, Harry Edwards and, of course,
the ever helpful team at Shire.
All photographs in this book are from the author's collection, excepting those on pages 17 (top), 19
(bottom right), 20 (centre), 21 (top right), 25 (bottom right), 27 (top right), which were taken at the
Cotswold Motoring and Toy Museum at Bourton-on-the-Water, and those on pages 17 (bottom two), 19
(top, centre left and bottom left), 22 (bottom right), 23 (centre), 24 (all), 34 (centre), which were taken at
the National Motor Museum, Beaulieu. The author wishes to acknowledge the help he received from
both museums. The photographs on page 45 appears by courtesy of Mike and Sue Richardson.

Printed and bound in Great Britain.

Contents

Model railway trucks of all makes, ages and gauges had the names of commercial companies on them to add realism. The petrol tanker was a common railway truck. This is another sideline to the collecting of petroleum artefacts.

Selling the petrol

In November 1895 J. A. Koosen imported a 5 horsepower Lutzmann car into Portsmouth. It is reported that he spent two days trying to start the car before he discovered that he needed petrol. This story gives some idea of the naivety of the early motorist and his unfamiliarity with petroleum spirit. The earliest known use of the word 'petrol' was in a letter from Eugen Langen to his friend Adolf Schmidt of Liège dated 28th September 1876. The first vehicle in England to be propelled by actual combustion was Edward Butler's tricycle, completed in 1888. Written on the rear mudguard were the words 'The petrol-cycle'.

It is generally agreed that it was the chemical-processing firm of Carless, Capel & Leonard of Hackney Wick in east London that first promoted the word and used it widely. Carless distilled heavy oil for lighting and heating and because there was no ready market for the light fuel left over it was sold off as cleaning fluid – petrol was at first a waste product! In 1893 Frederick Simms approached Carless, Capel & Leonard for fuel to use in the engines he was buying from Daimler in Germany, mainly for powering small boats. In that year he was ordering over 100 gallons (455 litres) a month of this cleaning fluid, now known as 'launch spirit'. When talking with William Leonard he commented that a name should be found for this product and suggested that the firm adopt the word 'petrol'. At first this was thought to be too close to 'petroleum', the trade name for paraffin oil, but Simms won the day. In a very long letter in the January 1897 edition of *Autocar*, Carless, Capel & Leonard refer to 'the special spirit petrol which we manufacture for use in motors'. Gradually the word came into common usage, though for some time Carless, Capel & Leonard had to fight other

Petrol was at first a by-product of lighting oil such as this Lighthouse oil manufactured by Carless, Capel & Leonard.

In a 1904 booklet Carless, Capel & Leonard was offering 'tanks suitable for storing petrol under licence'. The plate on the front says 'for use with light locomotives'. This was the phrase still being used in parliamentary terms for the motor vehicle. In the same booklet was advertised a Patent Benzine safety lamp for use in motor houses and places where cars and petrol were kept. It must be remembered that electric lighting was very uncommon at this time and a naked flame was extremely dangerous.

companies for it. It is interesting to note that during the two-gallon can era very few companies other than Carless used the word on their cans, preferring the term 'motor spirit'.

Before 1900 up to 40 gallons (182 litres) of petrol could be stored on premises provided it was in containers of 20 gallons (91 litres) or less. For more than 40 gallons the premises had to be licensed. An amendment to the 1896 Locomotives on the Highways Act, which came into force in May 1900, stipulated that vessels used for storing petrol were to be of a capacity 'not exceeding two gallons' (9 litres), otherwise the motorist would need to have a petroleum licence. At the same time up to 60 gallons (273 litres) (in two-gallon cans) could be kept in one place without a licence. This explains the standardisation by petrol companies on the two-gallon can.

Cans were usually delivered to the local railway station and collected from there by the customer. For the rich this was very similar to ordering special provisions from, say, Fortnum & Mason. Commercial suppliers received their petrol in the same way. Petrol could be bought at all sorts of premises: cycle shops, ironmongers, blacksmiths, chemists, grocers and hotels. The last were very quick to welcome motorists and to provide overnight facilities for them.

Carless, Capel & Leonard already had a chain of over 1500 outlets for their lighting and heating oil products and other chemicals, and many of these varied sources began stocking petrol. In the early years Carless had a virtual monopoly on selling this type of fuel but in 1898 the Standard Oil Company of America started marketing motor spirit through the Anglo American Oil Company.

As more and more petrol companies came into being, so they needed to attract the motorist to their particular product. Advertising became very important in all its forms, an example being the two-gallon can, neatly painted, often in bright colours, with the company name emblazoned on the side. As we shall see, almost anything produced by these early petrol companies had their name on it somewhere.

*'Petrol, what it is, where it may be obtained and
other information useful to autocarists'. In the early
days suppliers were few and often far between.
Carless produced a booklet with names and
addresses. Note the use of the word 'autocarists' for
motorists.*

Soon the cycle works, the blacksmiths and others turned their
business to looking after the needs of the motorist and became garages
or motor works. All would have sold petrol in cans. Some owners of
fleets of vehicles in the late 1900s had their petrol pumped from
underground tanks to their motors by a simple hand pump that did
not give an indication of the quantity dispensed. The first roadside
hand-operated pump in Britain is reputed to have been installed in
Shrewsbury in 1920, though such pumps had been in use in the United
States and on the Continent for a few years. Soon many of the garages
and some shops in towns and villages had hand-operated pumps. The
first electric petrol pumps were introduced in 1930, speeding up the
delivery of the fuel, though initially some motorists were worried about
the dangers of petrol and electricity being used in such close proximity.

Before long the need arose to supply petrol to motorists travelling
long distances away from urban areas. The Automobile Association
built the first roadside filling station at Aldermaston on the Bath Road
in Berkshire in 1920. Others soon followed. The main purpose of these
new premises was to sell petrol and oil. There was no need for elaborate
buildings; a corrugated iron shed would suffice to keep the staff out of
the weather. Petrol companies wanted to sell their brands in as many
outlets as possible and therefore these filling stations had many more

This postcard is captioned 'The longest filling station in the provinces'. At the Watling Street filling station there are at least ten pumps on the forecourt.

pumps than they needed. They were soon plastered with a great array of enamel advertising signs, each intended to attract the motorist to a particular company's pump. The Council for the Protection of Rural England and many others objected, considering these signs to be eyesores. In a booklet entitled *The Village Pump*, produced by the Design Industries Association, the garages are said to have been 'peppered with enamel signs of every colour and… the owner had these signs… almost forced upon him by agents of the petrol, oil and tyre companies… he pays nothing for them and gets nothing for their display'. Later many companies agreed to take down the signs but they made sure that their pumps were clearly painted in their corporate colours and had their name displayed on the globe on top.

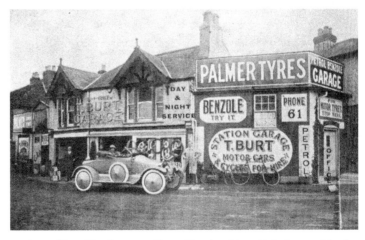

Station Garage at Totton, on the outskirts of Southampton. Covered in advertising, this is the sort of site that planners in urban areas and the Council for the Protection of Rural England and other similar bodies wished to eradicate. This is a letterpress advertising postcard with Mr T. Burt's name and telephone number on the reverse. The business was established in 1897 and this picture is probably from c.1914. It clearly advertises petrol for sale but no pumps are visible, so it is likely to predate the petrol pump era. In 2004 the gabled building was still standing, in a dilapidated condition but very recognisable.

This illustration comes from an advertising booklet published c.1922 by Pratts in conjunction with Gilbert & Barker, petrol-pump manufac-

turers. The pictures in it show a number of very early installations such as this one at Weybridge in Surrey. The booklet says in its introduction: 'Bulk storage ... the petrol consumers in the United Kingdom ought not to be behind the times in their handling of motor spirit, and there is no reason for this to be the case in the future.'

Soon many new filling stations took on an up-market look with, for example, Chinese pagoda styles or thatched cottage designs – a complete contrast with that which had been there before. Many stations attached cafés or tearooms to the site. It was not until after the Second World War that petrol companies started buying up sites in quantity or making deals with garage owners to sell only their products – the 'solus' or company-owned site is now universal.

The new style of filling station for the countryside – built of wood and thatched, supposedly to blend in with its surroundings. A café and bed and breakfast business has been incorporated in one and a tearoom in the other. The Haldon Thatch (top) is on the outskirts of Exeter on the road to Torbay and Plymouth. The Windmill Garage (bottom) is near Ringwood in Hampshire.

Two-gallon petrol cans

The standard two-gallon petrol can is one of the most collected of all petroleum items. Carless, Capel & Leonard at first used round two-gallon cans that tapered at the top. These were packed in threes in wooden boxes, usually to be distributed by rail. Other companies used similar cans, usually with an engraved plate on the side bearing the petrol company's name. Perhaps the first advertisement featuring the square two-gallon can – that of Pratts Motor Car Spirit – appeared in the *Autocar* of 5th January 1901. These cans were normally placed four to a crate for distribution.

Most two-gallon cans were made by Valor Limited and this name appears on the underside of the can along with the date of manufacture. Other manufacturers were Reads of Liverpool, Feaver & Company of London and Grant of London. The names and dates of manufacture of a non-Valor can are usually to be found on the uprights of the can handle or embossed on the top of the can, immediately under the handle. The machines and presses for making these cans were often supplied by Taylor & Challem Limited, engineers of Birmingham.

Cans always remained the property of the petroleum company and most carried an embossed message telling the user that a deposit had been paid on the can, and that it was to be returned to the suppliers.

The very first cans for selling petrol to the motorist were round and packed three into a wooden box for transit.

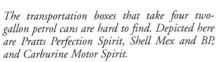

The transportation boxes that take four two-gallon petrol cans are hard to find. Depicted here are Pratts Perfection Spirit, Shell Mex and BP, and Carburine Motor Spirit.

Some collectors prefer to acquire the brass can tops as separate items from the cans. On the top row of this display are two unusual types that were tried as replacements for the castellated cap. In the third row down, second from right, is a top bearing an aeroplane and a monogram. The author has yet to see a can to go with this top.

Deposits started at 2s 6d in the earliest years and had reached 8 shillings by the end of the Second World War. It is apparent from the number of cans in collections and in circulation today that very many people lost their deposits! The name of the petrol company or owner of the can was always prominently embossed on the sides of the can and sometimes also on the top.

Until around 1915 the pouring outlet was 1 inch (25 mm) in diameter, after which it changed to 1½ inches (38 mm). All cans had a brass cap, usually with the company's name on it. This cap was castellated to ease unscrewing. To avoid the

have been made to stock Mex Motor Spirit at most of the boat houses and hotel garages along the river.

The clean, powerful character of the spirit, its speed-producing quality and its unfailing uniformity all make for efficient and economical running. Mex is "the brand you need for miles and speed."

THE MEX PATENT "OPEN-EASY" FAUCET.

In view of the difficulty and trouble experienced in opening the ordinary type of faucet, the Bowring Petroleum Co. has introduced a patent "open-easy" faucet, which is illustrated herewith. This device obviates the necessity for tools to open the can. With Mex Spirit a touch of the thumb and finger releases the patent "open-easy" faucet, and the pure petrol from the wells of Mexico is instantly at the service of the motorist.

THE OLD WAY   THE NEW WAY

OF OPENING SPIRIT CANS

THE BOWRING PETROLEUM C⁰ Lᵀᴰ Finsbury Court, LONDON e.c.

Some people found it difficult to open the petrol cans with castellated caps; certainly it could be tricky if you did not have a suitable tool. Mex introduced a cap (or faucet) that was undone by turning a butterfly-type screw. In a booklet Mex described this device as 'a patent "open easy" faucet [that] obviates the necessity for tools to open the can'. To back up its claim, the company issued a postcard (this one postmarked 1916) showing the 'old way' and the 'new way'.

Examples of a number of tools especially developed to help the motorist undo the castellated cap on a petrol can.

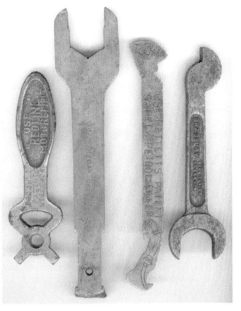

content being tampered with, the petrol cap was wired to the can and fastened with a lead seal. Special tools embossed with the petrol company's name were supplied to aid the removal of the cap. These tools helped prevent damage to the can. To assist pouring, accessory manufacturers offered easy-pour spouts made of brass, some being quite elaborate and fitted with flexible tubing for use on difficult tanks. Many petrol tanks were positioned under the bonnet and quite high up, thus making it awkward to pour in the petrol from a can. To overcome this problem, the petrol companies and others offered large funnels for use by garages and suppliers or by private individuals. These were usually square rather than round, and the petrol company's name was always displayed prominently on the side.

There were a few varieties of the standard two-gallon can. One of the more collectable is the can in which was placed a quart (1.1 litre) oil can. These were made predominantly for

'Girls fastening and sealing the green cans' is the title of this illustration from the 'Anglo American Journal' of January 1920. Once filled, the can was fitted with a numbered seal affixed by a wire.

Shell produced a two-gallon can that also contained an oil canister. Such cans are much sought after by collectors. When Shell and BP joined forces, the petrol was sold as BP and the oil as Shell.

Ross Petrol was an early supplier in Scotland, based in Glasgow before the First World War. The author has seen an advertisement for Ross Motor Spirit that features a can, but he has never seen such a can and wonders whether any still exist.

Shell. Because the oil can was not exposed to knocks in use, these are often to be found in very good condition and give the collector a good idea of the standard of finish of the original petrol can. BP (British Petroleum) had a similar can, but in this case the oil and its container came from Shell, presumably after the Shell and BP companies had merged.

Collectors have catalogued between 250 and 300 different two-gallon cans, but new names are being found all the time. The majority were produced by the petrol companies, for example Shell, Pratts, Redline, ROP (Russian Oil Products), National Benzole, Cleveland, Power and Regent. Not so well known were manufacturers such as BV & Company, Flight, Phoenix, Youngs, Giant, Ross and Bluebird. Large organisations, including Cadbury, United Dairies, the General Post Office and the Metropolitan Police, produced cans with their names on to try to prevent them being stolen. Another, Hebble Motor Spirit, was the

A selection of rare two-gallon cans from the author's collection. This display includes MG and Singer, which were manufactured especially for these makes of car, and Vulcan, a maker of both cars and commercial vehicles. Note the one that says 'Stolen from Fitzpatrick & Son'. The Racing Shell can (bottom row, second from right) is a reminder that petrol companies used motor-racing as a way of advertising to the motorist that their petrol was 'track tested'.

Some two-gallon cans were sold without any company name on them for use purely as spares. This unusual example would have been sold in accessory shops and garages. It has a triangular section at the back that slots into the can itself and is for holding spare oil.

property of Halifax's leading bus company. Two or three firms added a touch of humour, for example 'Stolen from McAlpine' or 'Stolen from Fitzpatrick'. Car manufacturers such as Singer, MG and Vulcan supplied cans with their name on the side.

It should be remembered that the can was used not only for the supply of petrol in the days before the petrol pump; many motorists would carry at least one two-gallon can, often mounted on the running board of their car, for spare petrol. Albert Lusty, who had a petrol round in the Cheltenham area and sold cans from the back of a light van, even had his own can. Examples of such local companies are very rare. Cans were also sold for other purposes; some had 'water only' or 'foam compound' embossed on them, to give two examples.

Perhaps the most frequently asked question about cans is what colour they should be. This is also the most difficult question to answer as cans were originally given only a very thin coat of paint. Those that survive are usually a sort of grey and are rather battered, and it is impossible to see an original colour. There is a tendency to over-restore the petrol can using modern thick paint, whereas the original coat was very thinly applied. As we have seen, there were many companies producing petroleum spirit, all vying for the attention of the motorist, and two-gallon cans were a petrol company's advertising statement. The cans were brightly coloured and were kept in excellent condition. Each can was checked when it came back to the fuel depot. It was cleaned inside and out and in many cases was rubbed down and a new

The Glico stand at the Motor Show at Olympia in 1920. This photographic postcard shows that the firm was offering three different brands of petrol to the motorist. The Glico name comes from the initials of the company, shown over the stand. On the reverse of the card is a Carburine Motor Spirit calendar for the twelve months commencing October 1920.

The can and can-box refurbishment programme was massive and the scale of it can be seen in this 1920 photograph taken at the Anglo American plant at Silvertown, above Woolwich Reach, London.

coat of paint applied, the petrol companies issuing booklets of detailed instructions to the painters. Similar attention was given to the wooden boxes in which the cans were despatched. No sets of paint samples survive so the collector has to look for other clues as to colour. Unfortunately colour advertisements, garage and petrol company letterheads, advertising postcards and other such publicity materials usually suffer from the vagaries of cheap colour printing.

Early cans, such as those of Pratts and Carburine, had paper panels stuck on one end and these were renewed each time the can came back to the depot. These panels lost popularity before the First World War, though Carburine used them again later. They are now very rare. In the early days petrol companies made only one grade of petrol. Later, when different grades were introduced, they used the same cans but painted them in different colours. Cans were painted vertically in two colours until after the First World War, when it

These advertising postcards for Pratts Perfection Spirit clearly show the paper panels attached to the ends of the early cans. Cans with any vestige of an original paper label are now very hard to find.

To denote a new grade of petrol, companies would sometimes paint their cans in two colours, vertically. This practice is clearly shown here on a Shell letterhead printed for J. Wadhams of Sonning, who advertised himself as a shoeing smith. It is interesting that he prefers the horse connection to that with the motor car. This entire bill is for items to do with shoeing horses.

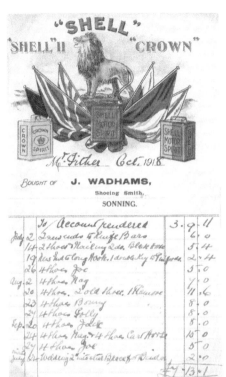

became commonplace for a different can to be produced for each grade. Genuine two-colour cans are now very rare indeed.

Most petrol companies sold oil as well. Car engines were much looser than they are these days and used a lot of oil. Many two-gallon cans were emblazoned with the names of oil companies and oil grades, just as were the petrol cans. As with petrol, local companies provided their own cans, Roys of Wroxham, a Norfolk department store, being one such example. Soon it was found necessary to sell oil in larger and smaller containers. The five-gallon oil can (22.7 litres) with conical top was popular and in later years many were lavishly decorated with racing scenes; one by Gamage (a London department store), for example, is very collectable. Then came the disposable can from one pint (0.57 litre) upwards. Printed on tin, these were often very attractive and, again,

Left: *In February 1899 Charles Cheers Wakefield took the greatest risk of his life. He resigned from Vacuum Oil (later to become Mobil Oil) to form his own company, C. C. Wakefield & Company, which later became Castrol. This heavy five-gallon can was an early container for Wakefield's oil. 'Return when empty to Crown Wharf, Hayes, Middlesex, GWR' is a reminder that the lubricant was usually transferred by rail.*

Above: *Many oil cans were highly pictorial, as these two from ROP (Russian Oil Products) and the department store Gamage show. They convey the message that the product can safely be used in transport that travels by land, sea or air. Motor-racing adds another dimension to the theme.*

These miniature cans (back row) were designed for use on children's pedal cars. The smaller cans would hold liquid but their purpose is not known. The central can (front) is the White Rose lamp oil can with a paper panel announcing that it contained perfume for representatives to give away at Christmas.

some bore pictorial images. A number of cans were produced specifying the makes of car in which they could be used, for example Trojan, BSA, Lanchester and Daimler.

Never wanting to miss a trick, some petrol companies produced miniatures of the two-gallon can for use on the running boards of children's pedal cars, usually made by Lines Brothers under the Triang name. Even some Minic clockwork toys had a very small can on them. Miniature petrol cans were also used in garages to sell or give away lighter fuel to customers and at Christmas the White Rose lamp oil company even produced its own brand of perfume in miniature cans for its representatives to give to their wives!

The two-gallon can still has many uses. Some readers may have one in their tool shed full of petrol for the motorised lawnmower. Have another look at it – it might be a rare one!

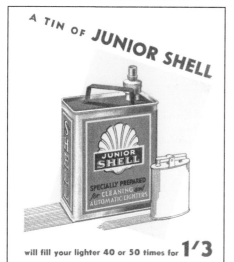

A TIN OF **JUNIOR SHELL**

will fill your lighter 40 or 50 times for **1′3**

Junior Shell is made from basic petrols which are skilfully blended to produce a balance of the necessary characteristics: to meet the needs of the smoker for a spirit that will light up readily and burn without any unpleasant smell or smoke, and for the housewife who must have an efficient stain remover which will leave no mark and no odour.

Junior Shell was an oil by-product made for lighters (and general cleaning) and was sold in small cans. Often these cans were placed on the counter in garages and one could either buy the whole can or fill one's lighter from it for 1d. Sometimes the fuel was available in little dispensers in the form of a pump.

The forecourt

Motorists often suspected that they were not getting the petrol product they had paid for. In this case the enamel sign refers to the underground storage tank being sealed by the petrol company's representative immediately after filling.

From 1920 onwards the forecourt of any garage or filling station was dominated by petrol pumps. These pumps were owned by the petrol companies, who, wishing to be well represented in all areas, installed more pumps on every forecourt than was necessary for passing trade.

The earliest pumps were imported from the United States and were hand-operated. All had some form of indicator on them to show the amount of petrol being dispensed. As always, the motorist was suspicious of the quantities being supplied. Soon pumps appeared with one or two graduated glass containers at the top into which the petrol was pumped. When the required gallonage was reached the petrol was released by gravity into the tank of the car. Weights and measures inspectors regularly checked the pumps but this was not enough for many motorists and so firms started advertising that their petrol came from a 'sealed pump' – in other words, no one could tamper with the settings. A number of companies highlighted 'filtered' petrol in their advertisements to reassure the customer that it was pure. When electric pumps were introduced in the

The British firm Beck was one of the more popular petrol-pump makers. These two pumps are to be found fully restored to working order in the historic garage project at the National Motor Museum. One has a clock-face dial and the other has numbers that are revealed in little apertures; one gives the running price of the petrol already pumped and the other the gallonage being dispensed.

A Pratts-supplied padlock, now a rare collector's item. This one is featured on a horse-drawn Anglo American tank distribution vehicle held in the stores of the Science Museum at Wroughton in Wiltshire.

1930s they all had a large dial at the front on which the gallonage could be checked.

Security at night was a problem. Most hand pumps had a cover at the front and often at the back that slid around to expose the pump handles and the dials. These were locked shut at night, often with a padlock supplied by the petrol company and so marked. Security on electric pumps was easier as the power could be cut off inside the building.

Some urban garage owners wanted to place a pump on the pavement outside their premises. To do so required the permission of the local authority. One authority required the owner to keep the pump in good condition and to ensure that it was illuminated from lighting-up time until 11 p.m. He was charged a rent of 5 shillings per year for this privilege, though some councils charged as much as £20 per year. To overcome this many garage owners placed the pump

Stour Garage in Church Street, Shipston-on-Stour, Warwickshire, has a number of pumps against the wall of its premises. Petrol is delivered to cars at the kerbside by means of the overhead swinging arm, which extends over the pavement out of the way of pedestrians.

Here at Glenluce in Scotland a trader has erected a petrol pump in the centre of the pavement. No doubt the owner paid an annual rent to the local council for this.

A Bowser hand-operated petrol pump converted for serving petrol after hours with the Brecknell Slot Automatic Petrol conversion. The instructions are: 'Do not use damaged coins. Before inserting 1/- handle must be turned back as far as possible. Insert 1/- in hole in front of handle. Turn in this direction (diagram alongside).' One imagines this was very much an emergency supply as the carrying of spare cans of petrol was commonplace.

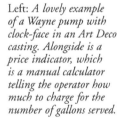

on their own premises but fitted it with a swinging arm that reached out over the pavement above head height, thus allowing the car to be filled up at the kerbside. In order to sell petrol out of hours, a few garages adopted a system of 'slot automatic petrol', marketed by Brecknell, Munro & Rogers, whereby the motorist could serve himself by putting shilling coins into the slot. These pumps were never particularly successful and are now very difficult to find.

With the petrol pump came the petrol globe – an internally lit glass advertising sign that sat neatly on top of the pump. The Shell pecten is probably the best-known, designed by Stanley Wilson in 1915. Most globes were made of one piece of milk glass and were round or square with the petrol company's logo on them; some, such as Redline's, were triangular

Above: *The Shell pecten is probably the most recognisable of all petrol company logos. It is depicted here on a petrol pump globe of the early 1930s.*

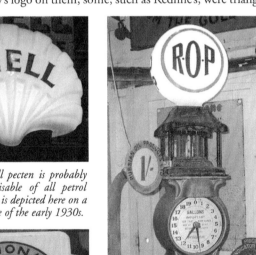

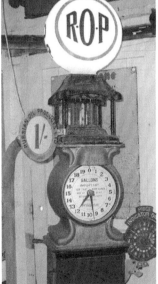

Left: *A lovely example of a Wayne pump with clock-face in an Art Deco casting. Alongside is a price indicator, which is a manual calculator telling the operator how much to charge for the number of gallons served.*

Left: *The winged head of Mercury on a petrol pump globe of National Benzole.*

This petrol pump globe was sold in 1998 as a collector's item – for a world record price of £16,500. Coalene Mixture was a petrol processed from coal. The Royal Air Force ran most of its aeroplanes on this fuel until the Second World War. A lot of experimentation took place to make petrol from coal in an attempt to make the United Kingdom less dependent on imported fuels.

or other odd shapes. Because petrol globes were made of glass they have not survived in large numbers and are very much in demand by collectors. On the forecourt additional illuminated globes were often mounted on simple structures away from the pumps to act as advertising signs to attract motorists.

Below: It was a legal requirement for the price of petrol to be displayed. This is another example of a petrol company declaring that its tanks have been sealed after delivery.

By law all petrol pumps had to display clearly the price per gallon. Each company had its own way of doing this, but the price indicator was usually in the form of a metal holder that clipped on to the pump. Many of these have survived. Those for Shell were often shell-shaped. BP's took the form of the company's Union Jack logo, with the price mounted in the centre. Redline's were triangular, whilst Regent Ethyl had metal price tags that slotted in and could be easily changed. Most, however, consisted of cardboard pricing labels displayed behind glass or perspex. All had the petrol company's name around the edge.

The clutter of pumps at the roadside was one of the eyesores that critics tried to do away with. The pump-maker Theo came up with the design for a pump, the Theo Multiple Pump, that could draw petrol from up to six different underground tanks, each with its own brand of fuel, so that one pump would do the job of six. Both the hand-operated and the electric Theo are now very much sought after.

Motorists required oil – often as much as a pint (0.57 litre) at every fill-up. Oil was usually supplied to a garage in barrels; sometimes

Brimfield Filling Station, Herefordshire, 1931, from an old postcard. All the old clutter around the site has gone and there is now just one pump, a Theo Multiple, which provides six different makes or grades of petrol. The cars in view are a Riley and an Essex.

Left: *Advertising photographs for the Theo Multiple Pump, both in hand-operated and electric form (the former with a round petrol globe and the latter with a square one). Each pump clearly shows the list of six petrol makes that can be served from it. The hand-operated pump assures the motorist of 'spirits guaranteed not to mix'. Both pumps have indicators to tell the motorist which make of petrol is being served.*

Above: *Every Theo Multiple Pump was sold with its own petrol globe. As it was selling a number of different makes and grades of petrol, such a pump could not display the globe of any one company. Theo globes are rare items to find.*

Here at the Studland Motor Depot in Dorset National Benzole and Pratts petrol are sold from the pumps. On the left of the forecourt is a display of Shell petrol in cans. In the centre are two barrels dispensing Mobil Oil with the aid of simple hand pumps mounted on top of the barrel. There is also an upturned barrel with a pump on top. To the side of the garage are two enamel signs (backs to the camera), which look as if they have recently been removed, possibly to satisfy the planners or objectors.

Left and below: Sterns Limited of Finsbury Square, London, was an early company providing oils and greases under the names of Sternol and Sterntrac. The firm also produced an oil, Loroline, especially for steam lorries. The cat theme was continued on a number of advertising items including a set of playing cards, 'the lure of the purr'. Sterns also gave away a tape-measure bearing the company name, as well as pouring cans and oil cans.

Type 63

THE WAKEFIELD DRUM CABINET

For Three 10-Gallon Drums

Taps are supplied with this outfit to fit in the bung-hole of drums and are fastened by means of hooks which engage under the curved lip. When the fly-nuts are unscrewed the hooks are free to swing, and are then held in position while the fly-nut is tightened. Care must be taken that the tap is fitted with outlet in the downward position. When tap has been fitted the drum should be placed on its side ready to insert in the cabinet. The drum should then be punctured on the top side at the bottom end of the drum as a vent for air, and placed in position. This cabinet can also be supplied with two shelves for tins in place of the top drum, or with six shelves for tins instead of drums.

Size : Height 5' 6" (plus height of chart 15½") × 2' 0½" deep × 1' 6½" wide.

Type No. 63, for three 10-gallon drums, complete with three taps and tray for measures -	£8 0 0
Type No. 632, for two 10-gallon drums, complete with two taps and two shelves for tins -	£8 0 0
Type No. 636, with six shelves for tins -	£7 0 0

Net. Carriage paid any station U.K.

OPEN

CLOSED—Showing Grade Transfers.

Left: The Castrol cabinet as illustrated in a trade brochure dated June 1927. Here the ten-gallon drums of oil are concealed in a neat cabinet that has a multiple of transfers on it. Such cabinets are very difficult to find these days with their original transfers in place. Some good examples of similar restored and unrestored cabinets are to be found at the National Motor Museum in Beaulieu. An unrestored example is depicted below.

How to buy oil!
~cheaper
~cleaner
~quicker

SHELL MOTOR OIL

Above: A charming advertisement for Shell oil, showing the oil cabinet with the hand pump delivering from a concealed tank in the base. This was in the days when an attendant served the motorist!

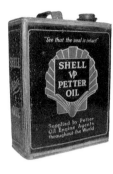

Oil was sold for many purposes other than lubricating motor vehicles. This is a special brand of Shell oil produced for Petter oil engines, a popular make of portable power sources, much used by farmers. It would have been stocked by the local garage as well as by specialist suppliers. 'See that the seal is intact' is another reminder that purchasers were wary of the possibility of the product having been tampered with.

these barrels stood on the forecourt with a small hand pump attached but usually they were encased in a cabinet provided by the oil companies. There were often enamel notices on the cabinet saying that all advertising had to be removed if a different make of oil was being dispensed. Later came the oil cabinet with an integral tank and fixed hand pump on top, usually entirely enclosed with a cover that came down at night, secured by the company padlock. Whilst it was normally possible to mount the oil cabinets permanently, some were built as a tank and pump on wheels. These could be taken in at night and brought out by day. They were also useful where there was a need to take oil to the vehicles, and they had a good following in boatyards. Oil was usually dispensed into one- or two-pint tin pourers, always emblazoned with the oil company's name. All such pouring cans had on them a seal to show that they had been checked by a weights and measures inspector when new and that the cost of this inspection was included in the price at which they were sold. Oil was sold in smaller

A tinplate sign showing prices for Castrol oil.

	½ PINT	1 PINT	1 QUART	3 PINTS	½ GALLON	5 PINTS	¾ GALLON	7 PINTS	1 GALLON
PATENT CASTROL CW&AA	6ᵈ	11ᵈ	1/8	2/6	3/4	4/2	4/11	5/7	6/3
PATENT CASTROL XL	7ᵈ	1/1	2/-	3/-	3/11	4/9	5/7	6/5	7/2
PATENT CASTROL C	7ᵈ	1/-	1/10	2/8	3/6	4/4	5/2	6/-	6/8
PATENT CASTROL XXL	8ᵈ	1/2	2/3	3/4	4/4	5/2	6/-	6/10	7/8
PATENT CASTROL R	9ᵈ	1/4	2/6	3/10	5/-	6/2	7/2	8/2	9/2

WAKEFIELD MEASURES

The Quart, Pint and Half-Pint Certified Measures are robustly made in heavy gauge tin-plate for use with all Wakefield Tanks, Barrel and Drum Cabinets.

Quart Measure	Pint Measure	Half-Pint Measure
2/6	2/-	1/6

The set of three Measures - 5/-

(The price includes L.C.C. Stamping Fee)

Pouring cans for measures of one quart (1.1 litres) and one pint (0.57 litre), both available from Castrol. The illustration is from a trade brochure.

Left: A rack of almost perfect conical oil cans by Castrol from the late 1930s. These are on display at the National Motor Museum in Beaulieu and came originally from Tucker's Garage at Wedmore, Somerset, where Jack Tucker had neatly replaced all the empty cans in their original cardboard boxes, to be found by the Museum over fifty years later!

Right: This Redex upper-cylinder lubricant dispenser is a very neat item. The miniature jug is filled by a few pushes on the brass plunger on the right. The dispenser is refilled by removing the cap on the left.

tins (see the previous chapter) but by the late 1930s the oil bottle was becoming common; these are now collector's items.

It was thought that upper-cylinder lubricant prolonged the life of an engine. Redex is possibly the most familiar name but Shell and Mobil also produced versions. Other makes included Castrollo by Castrol, Citex by Chemco and Motorine by Price. All had small metal containers encircling a dispenser from which a measure could be obtained. For many years it cost a penny to add a measured amount of upper-cylinder lubricant to every 2 gallons (9.1 litres) of petrol.

Even after the petrol pump became commonplace two-gallon petrol cans were displayed on the forecourt, mostly for brands or blends not available at the pumps. These cans were usually placed on a display stand provided by the petrol company and bearing its name. Water was another important commodity to the motorist. Water cans on the forecourt tended to be similar to galvanised garden cans but many had

the badge of a petrol company on them. Petrol companies also produced non-petroleum items for the motorist such as antifreeze.

There is another type of petrol pump that is often traded amongst collectors today. This is a simple hand pump, sometimes with a dial, sometimes without. Unlike the forecourt pump, it has no casing. These 'skeleton' or 'yard' pumps were for use by private individuals or firms that served a fleet of vehicles and were mounted on the firm's premises, feeding from an underground tank. It was not uncommon to find them dispensing paraffin at the back of a garage or service station.

The 'yard' or 'skeleton' pump was a simple hand-operated pump for use by farmers, hauliers and others who had small fleets of vehicles but wanted a bulk underground tank. In this case one is set up for filling cans with paraffin for distribution in the local area. Paraffin was used for heating and cooking long after electricity had reached rural areas.

Petrol advertising

Within motoring collections there is likely to be a selection of the enamel signs that decorated the walls of the garage or showroom. The enamel sign became popular in the 1890s and in the first years of the twentieth century a number of motoring and petrol company advertisements appeared. For the petroleum collector the period 1920–39 was the heyday of the enamel sign, though because of the unpopularity of such advertising, particularly in Britain, many signs were removed in the 1930s.

Some motoring signs are very attractive and vie for popularity with the best signs for other products. Signs relating to the sale of petrol and oil seem to be dull by comparison. Few are pictorial, an exception being 'The Winner – The British Petrol', a large sign featuring a racing car crossing the finishing line at speed. Most petroleum signs are simple statements of fact such as 'Price's Motor Oils', 'Wakefield Castrol Motor Oil', 'We Sell Sealed Shell' and 'Get Pratts Here'. Some just name the make of petrol and give the price per gallon alongside (inflation was so low that a change of price was quite rare). Not all signs were flat; some were small and designed to stick out from a wall. Some simply provided an excuse to advertise the name while promoting a different service. For example, many garages had cars for hire or ran a taxi service, hence the sign 'Shell – Cars for Hire'. There were many variations on the enamel sign, one of the most popular being the 'Duckhams Adcoids' advertisement in the form of a thermometer. While most were to be found around garages and filling stations, there were enamel signs all over a town, and particularly alongside a railway or on a railway station.

Left: *A lovely enamel sign for Power petrol depicting the Power globe. Both this sign and the actual globe are now very hard to find.*

Right: *This is one of the most pictorial enamel advertising signs for petrol. Unlike the manufacturers of many other everyday products, petrol companies were keener on words than on illustrations.*

Petrol companies would often contrive a connection between aeroplane fuel and motor fuel – indeed in many cases it was the same – as it was commonly held that if it was reliable enough for an aeroplane it must certainly be good in a car. This enamel sign dates from before the petrol pump. The golden-coloured can was Shell Aviation Motor Spirit.

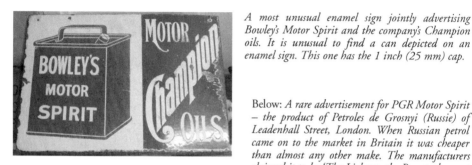

A most unusual enamel sign jointly advertising Bowley's Motor Spirit and the company's Champion oils. It is unusual to find a can depicted on an enamel sign. This one has the 1 inch (25 mm) cap.

Below: A rare advertisement for PGR Motor Spirit – the product of Petroles de Grosnyi (Russie) of Leadenhall Street, London. When Russian petrol came on to the market in Britain it was cheaper than almost any other make. The manufacturers claimed it to be 'The Lightest, the Purest, the most Powerful, and most Economical Spirit on the British market'.

This very unusual early Pratts advertisement is from a book and features one of the company's own enamel signs. Another version of this sign depicts a veteran-style car in the corner.

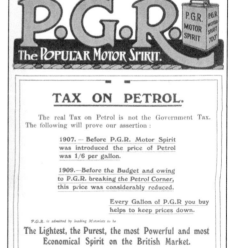

A large sign informing the motorist that he is approaching a garage in which he can fill up with Pratts petrol. Many garages offered cars for hire, usually with driver, so this fact was often included on the enamel signs. The Shell Mex globe alongside the sign would have been mounted away from the pumps; the arrow shows the motorist the way to the Shell pump.

When they had outlived their usefulness many old signs were used to patch up garden sheds, bolster coal bunkers or make walls for compost heaps on allotments. They can still be found in the most unusual situations.

Throughout the 1920s and 1930s one company, Shell, stood out for the standard of its advertising and posters. In the 1920s it produced a wide selection of posters, measuring 30 by 40 inches (76 by 102 cm), known as 'lorry bills'. Shell had a large fleet of lorries out on the road, providing a wonderful opportunity for mobile billboards, with a poster on each side and one at the rear. Shell's early advertising often included a car and a motorcycle alongside a petrol pump and a petrol can. These advertisements were designed to remind the motorist which can to buy or which pump to fill up at on the forecourt. The company then developed a series of posters based on the theme of visiting the countryside. This included a wide range of scenes with the overall title of 'See Britain First on Shell'. Virtually none of these posters features anything remotely to do with the selling of Shell petrol. Another popular series was

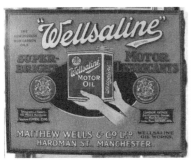

Left: Enamel signs are usually in a damaged state when found. Almost perfect enamels such as this one for Wellsaline Motor Oil are very hard to find.

This well-known Shell advertisement by Rene Vincent provides a good example of a pump with the globe on top and the price label on the side. Petrol was pumped up into the two glass containers at the top and then released by gravity. Some petrol could be left in the pipe, so the attendant is about to lift it up to extract the last drop. The car even has a Shell radiator mascot!

'Visiting the Countryside with Shell', a lorry bill by Eric George. There is no sign of a car, a petrol pump, a garage or a road festooned with telegraph poles – nothing other than the wording tells you that this is a petrol advertisement.

Right: One of a series of lorry bills produced by Shell depicting various types of people who 'prefer Shell'. In this poster by the American painter Charles Shaw it is smokers who prefer Shell. The series included gardeners, seamen, anglers, artists, architects and many more.

Pratts produced a whole series of humorous postcards, many similar to the saucy seaside variety as in this example.

Sternol Oil was prominent in the advertising game. Here are two of a series of advertising postcards produced by the company. On the reverse was a Sternol flag flying from a flagpole with the message 'The standard of excellence'. There was also a drawing of Windsor Castle.

given over to different groups of workers under the caption 'These Men Use Shell' and another memorable series featured the slogan 'That's Shell That Was'. Twice a year Shell produced a different poster advising the motorist to change from Winter to Summer Shell Oil and vice versa. These lorry bills were originally intended to last only a short time but some were never displayed at all and these now command high prices at auction. Shell also had an excellent set of advertising postcards.

It is difficult to collect petroleum advertising from newspapers and

Shell was a prolific producer of advertising postcards. Here are four varied ones. 'Helping Father, the right thing in the wrong place' shows a boy standing on a two-gallon can box emptying the petrol into the radiator whilst an aviator seems determined to commit suicide stealing a motorist's can!

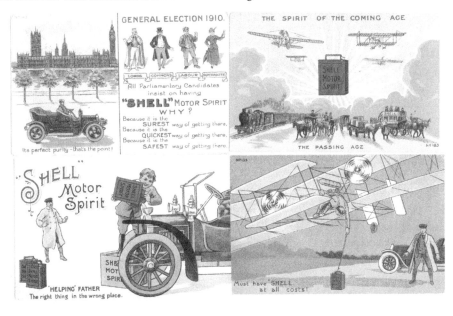

Above: *Bowring Petroleum, owner of Mex petrol, produced a number of advertising postcards. The one on the right has on its reverse 'The Brand you need, for miles and speed'. The artist has signed himself 'John de G. Bryan' but is actually 'The Motor' magazine's famous illustrator Bryan de Grineau.*

Right and below: *Donald McGill was very famous for illustrating a huge number of the classic saucy seaside postcards. Here he turns his humour on the pavement-mounted petrol pump, no doubt also taking into account the double entendre of the petrol company's name. The message on the reverse of the card (posted 24th December 1926) includes the following: 'from a grateful patient whose tank arrangements disturbed your "eat" of a year ago'. The mind boggles! The other card is one of the very well-known series published by Bamforth & Company of Holmfirth; it too was posted in 1926.*

Castrol has always been strong in sponsoring motor sport and other forms of competition in which its oil products are used. In 1912 the company produced the booklet 'From the Skyway and the Highway', which recorded some of its successes. This was later renamed 'Castrol Achievements' and was still being published in Castrol's centenary year of 1999. Highly pictorial, 'Castrol Achievements' is a very collectable series, especially the pre-war issues such as this one from 1934.

magazines; because of the paper it is printed on it is often of inferior quality. However, it is worth trying to find examples of this type of advertising in order to look at the content. A Motor Show catalogue from the 1920s or 1930s will contain a number of advertisements for petrol-pump manufacturers. Just as at Motor Shows car manufacturers would give away catalogues that are now avidly collected, so petrol and oil companies would prepare such material for distribution at trade shows. These trade leaflets often contain a wealth of background information about the ways in which petroleum products were sold; a number of them have been used as illustrations in this book.

Three words that occur frequently in petrol advertising require further explanation: 'anti-knock', 'anti-pinking' and 'ethyl'. Motor manufacturers were continually trying to improve the efficiency of their engines and wanted higher compression ratios within the cylinders to give more power. The higher

When a speed record was broken or an important race won using a particular brand of petrol or oil, the company was always quick to exploit the success. Castrol put a lot of money into sponsoring record attempts such as Malcolm Campbell's speed record of 301.13 mph (484.52 km/h) in Bluebird at Bonneville Salt Flats in September 1935. The illustrator is Bryan de Grineau, whose work appeared regularly in 'The Motor' magazine.

A simple-looking advertising card for Shell, celebrating Parry Thomas's land speed record in his car Babs at Pendine on 27th April 1926. Shell rather understated its own success because the speed reached was actually 169.30 mph (272.40 km/h). The following day Thomas did even better, raising the record to 171.02 mph (273.56 km/h). In this early example of paper engineering, as one opens the shell a small cardboard cut-out of Babs speeds across the right-hand page of the card.

compression ratios without better fuels tended to cause detonation that was known as 'pinking' or 'knocking', both of which could be harmful to an engine. Raising the octane rating of the petrol would overcome this and the addition of tetraethyl-lead-ethyl ('ethyl' for short) was one way of achieving this. Most companies widely advertised the fact that they added ethyl to their products. Pratts took this further than most by treating the product as if it were a girl called Ethel. Later alcohol was used in the form of methyl alcohol to achieve the same result; Cleveland Discol, for example, advertised it had an alcohol content.

A number of examples of trade materials aimed at the garage owner rather than the general public. The contents of this type of booklet give very useful background information for the collector.

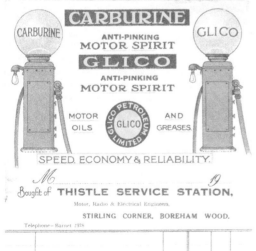

An invoice for the Thistle Service Station of Boreham Wood, Hertfordshire, printed and provided by Glico. Reference is made to 'anti-pinking'. Much was made by petrol companies of the abilities of their fuels to avoid pre-ignition or pinking.

Many experiments took place to find a way of making petrol out of coal. If successful this might have made Britain a little less dependent on imported fuel and would also have given work to a depressed mining industry. The first successful attempt was achieved as a by-product of Coalite, and Carless, Capel & Leonard obtained an agreement to refine this as motor fuel. Jack Leonard of Carless, never one to miss a trick, persuaded the Royal Air Force to run its fighters on the product. In 1935 Carless started selling Coalene to the motorist from a pump at Brew Brothers in Gloucester Terrace, London. Because the octane rating could not be increased Coalene production ceased in 1939, just when it was needed most.

Pratts used the word 'Ethyl' to denote a lady, as this advertising leaflet clearly shows. On the back is reproduced a letter from pioneer motorist S. F. Edge saying how he gets 'Better climbing – higher mileage – cleaner running on Pratts Ethyl petrol' in his six-cylinder AC car (25th February 1928).

Carless, Capel & Leonard was the first company to break into the petrol retailing business. By the 1930s its products were marketed as Carless. This globe, from the company's own collection, now at the National Motor Museum in Beaulieu, Hampshire, is from the 1930s.

This Gilbarco pump dispenses petrol via a swinging arm that extends out over the pavement. It probably originated as one owned by Pratts, but when the company was taken over by Esso in 1935 the petrol was rebranded – though Esso still felt it necessary to push the fact that it contained ethyl.

Other collectables

As we have seen, petrol companies were very keen on promoting themselves to garage and filling-station owners and to their customers and they produced a vast amount of promotional material.

Among the paper ephemera were maps. Possibly the best-known and the most attractive were those produced by Pratts Hightest, drawn by A. E. Taylor in about 1930, which were always intended for wall decoration rather than for general use. They were pictorial and covered such subjects as the Great North Road, the Bath Road, Watling Street, the New Forest, Scotland, Wales and Ireland. Many companies, including Mex, Pratts and ROP (Russian Oil Products), produced folding maps for use in the car. Pratts also made a most attractive board game in the form of a race at Brooklands (reissued by Esso in April 1935 when the company took over Pratts). Most companies seem to have asked J. Waddington to produce playing cards for them, the backs of which always carried an advertisement. Glico even produced a set of round playing cards. Shell was one of the companies to give away hand-held ball-rolling games, whilst Redline offered jigsaw puzzles.

Above: *Shell produced these advertising door plates for use in garages, workshops and filling stations. Good-quality printing on tin makes them an attractive item for the collector.*

One of the series of beautiful wall maps put out by Pratts in 1930. They are much sought after by collectors.

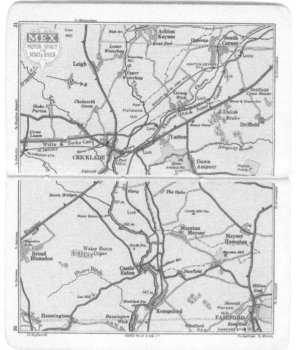

Many petrol companies produced maps for the motorist. This early one by Mex Motor Spirit of the River Thames and surrounding roads offered help to the motorist as well as the motor-boat owner. Mex Motor Spirit, marketed by Bowring Petroleum, was manufactured from product brought in from the oilfields of Mexico.

Three boxes or covers from sets of playing cards given away by petrol companies. The pack of Shell cards (top left) is in a leather-style book with fastener. The Shell Motor Spirit box is made to look like a can. The round cards at the bottom are by Glico – they must have been difficult to hold!

Packs of playing cards were popular items for petrol companies to use as advertising. Here are nine examples of the backs of such cards.

Anyone lucky enough to find an old garage that has lain undisturbed for many years will probably find the owner's desk full of very collectable items such as petrol companies' and other suppliers' letterheads. Many companies provided their retailers with notepaper and invoices for their own use that were overprinted with the proprietor's name and address. Many such sheets would have been filled in with pen and ink, so the blotter was important and the companies produced postcard-size blotters in several different forms, all carrying the company name. Each year the petrol companies sent

The office of a long-disused country garage might look something like this. In this recreation of 1938 at the National Motor Museum at Beaulieu everything on display is genuine and comes from a number of different garage clearouts. There are dozens of items of paper ephemera that refer to petrol and oil companies.

Within the office space of the historic garage recreation at the National Motor Museum is an area devoted to the sale of all sorts of motoring and other commodities. There are a number of oil and petrol products around the building and on the shelves – even old enamel signs to stop the stove from scorching the walls of the wooden building!

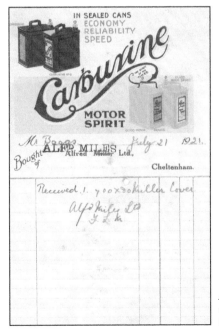

During both world wars the petrol companies 'pooled' their products, which were all marketed by the Pool Board as war spirit; it was known as Pool Petrol. This invoice for war spirit in December 1917 is a very rare item.

out desk and pocket diaries. One of the smallest pocket diaries measures 3.2 by 2.2 inches (8 by 5.5 cm) and came from Redline in the 1920s. Desk calendars were an annual present. Garage proprietors were often sent pencils in little cases shaped rather like petrol pumps and PGR Motor Spirit distributed its own ruler. You could be

A very rare invoice from Carburine showing the 1920s cans with paper labels on the end. The Carburine slogan was 'The Spirit of the Times'.

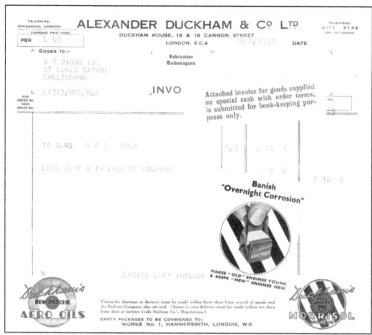

This Alexander Duckham invoice from August 1937 uses the word 'Aero' for a new type of oil. Adcoids were tablets that were added to petrol to 'banish overnight corrosion'; it was claimed that the product 'makes old engines young and keeps new engines new'. Duckham's Morrisol oil was manufactured especially for Morris cars under the brand name of Sirrom ('Morris' spelled backwards).

serenaded by 'Songs of BP' on a small gramophone record or you could have your drinks with cocktail sticks provided by BP (manufactured by Bell Brothers, Goldsmiths & Watchmakers of Darlington). For collectors postcards and photographs are among the most popular paper items. Any number of postcards of street scenes, garages and petrol pumps are offered for sale at autojumbles, postcard fairs and other such events. They are very collectable and they are becoming much more expensive. Photographs are rarer than postcards and are especially sought after.

Smokers' requisites were provided in quantity by the petrol company. Pratts produced both a stylish cigarette case and a small tin that would hold five cigarettes. The latter sported a can on the front and a pump on the back and contained cigarettes specially manufactured by B. Muratti Son &

ROP (Russian Oil Products) was a cheap petrol that many motorists thought was not very good. Motorists and garage hands remember it as 'Rotten Old Petrol'. Whatever the quality of the petrol, the letter heading is most decorative.

Above left: *Though damaged by fire, this BP hanging advertising card is still a very collectable item. It is from the early years of the petrol pump, when the two-gallon can was also still in regular use.*

Above right: *A very rare desk advertising calendar given away by the Anglo Dutch Petroleum Company in 1928.*

A very small 1925 pocket diary produced by Redline. A page from the inside of the diary proudly proclaims that the company has a 'service station at Brooklands Race Track'.

A Redline wall calendar for 1922 with all the months intact. It is a collector's dream to find something as complete as this and in such good condition.

Company of London. Small tins of vestas or matches were provided by Bretts Ovaline, Pratts Motor Lubricant and Pilchers Caroyle. Power and others produced small book matches. The copper ashtrays of Pratts Perfection Motor Spirit are well known to enthusiasts but similar ones were also produced by Silvertown Lubricants and by Redline Motor Spirit with Union Petroleum. Bluebird petrol, which lasted only a few years, had a copper ashtray with a ceramic centre depicting a bluebird. Lighters were also popular gifts.

There was a large variety of penknives with petrol company names

A Redline lorry delivering petrol in the early 1920s. This 2–3 ton lorry is a c.1917 Austin 20 horsepower with four-cylinder engine and scuttle-mounted radiator. The transmission was by twin shafts to bevel gears in each rear wheel. This sort of photographic postcard can sometimes be found at collectors' fairs and in postcard auctions.

A Pratts lorry delivering both cans and bulk petrol. The advertisement on the side of the lorry records the success of 'Softly-Catch-Monkey', a powerful Lanchester owned by Jo Hanns and raced by Tony Bellingham-Smith in the President's Gold Plate on 4th August 1924 at Brooklands. The lorry is one of many former War Department vehicles that were reconditioned for resale after the First World War.

or logos on them, as well as lapel and cap badges and key fobs. Many companies produced mirrors with their logo; Redline even gave away a clothes brush. When you bought a new car from a dealer you would often find a circular enamel plaque on the dashboard displaying the dealer's name and exhorting you to fill your car only with a specific make of oil.

Toys provide another wide field of petroleum collectables. Most types of car or lorry, either in tinplate or diecast, have been depicted in miniature over the years and petrol companies made sure their names appeared on the sides of appropriate commercial vehicles, usually petrol tankers. There were miniature petrol

Book matches for Power petrol. Note the emphasis on 'anti-knock petrol'.

A Glico-supplied letterhead from the 1930s with the company slogan 'miles of smiles'. It reminds us that the employees who delivered the petrol were often in uniform with a peaked cap and cap badge. Cap and lapel badges are very collectable.

Five toy vehicles from the author's collection, all representing Shell petrol tankers. (Top) Triang, c.1935. (Centre) Wells-Brimtoy no. 41, c.1934. (Bottom left) German, probably Kellerman, c.1935. (Bottom right) Unknown small English maker, c.1934/5.

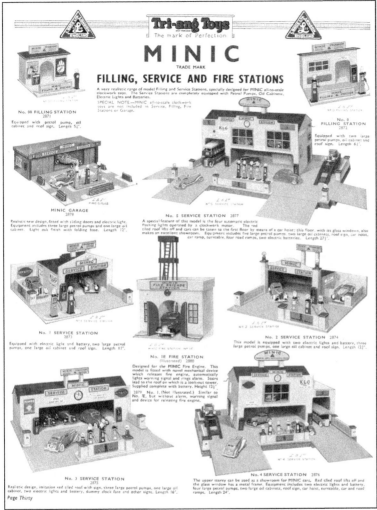

A page from a Triang toy catalogue of 1937 or 1938 showing some of the wide range of toy filling and service stations and garages made by this firm. There is a variety of petrol pumps with globes, oil cabinets and advertising enamels on offer.

pumps and oil cabinets, as well as toy garages of all sizes. Model railways would often feature a goods train with a petrol tank wagon bearing the name of Shell or Esso or some other company.

W. H. Goss, the manufacturer of Goss china souvenirs, usually displaying a town or place name or crest, and sold as mementoes of seaside holidays, also produced both a two-gallon petrol can and a Pratts Ethyl petrol pump in its series.

Further reading

Relatively little has been published on this subject in the United Kingdom. The following books all contain useful sections on petroleum collectables.

Baglee, Christopher, and Morley, Andrew. *Street Jewellery*. New Cavendish Books, 1988.

Baglee, Christopher, and Morley, Andrew. *Enamel Advertising Signs*. Shire, 2001.

Burgess-Wise, David. *Automobile Archaeology*. Patrick Stephens, 1981.

Gardener, Gordon, and Morris, Alistair. *Automobilia*. Antique Collectors Guide, 1982 and later editions. Includes price guides.

Hewitt, John. *The Shell Poster Book*. Profile Books, 1998.

Pugh, Peter. *Carless, Capel & Leonard plc*. Carless, Capel & Leonard, 1986.

Worthington-Williams, Mike. *Automobilia*. Batsford, 1979.

In the United States petroleum collectables are much bigger business. The following is just a small selection of books available.

Andreson, Scott. *Check the Oil*. Wallis-Homestead, 1986.

Lee, Bob. *Gilbert & Barker: Gilbarco Inc*. Harlo Press, 1989.

Lee, Bob. *S. F. Bowser*. Harlo Press, 1978.

Lee, Bob. *Ten Gallons for a Dollar: The History of the Gas Pump Companies and Service Stations*. Harlo Press, 1985.

Lee, Bob. *Tokheim Pump Company 1901–1980*. Harlo Press, 1980.

Schart, Jim, and Schart, Nancy. *American Automobilia*. Wallis-Homestead, 1994.

Stenzler, Mitch, and Pease, Rick. *Gas Station Collectables*. Schiffer Publishing, 1993.

Witzel, Michael Karl. *The American Gas Station*. Motor Books International, 1992.

This Pratt's illuminated sign is a very rare and unusual item. It has never been used and was being offered at a Beaulieu Autojumble complete with its wooden packing case.

Places to visit

Most of the museums of road transport in the United Kingdom have examples of petroleum collectables on display.

There are good examples of reconstructions of early garages in the museums listed below.

Beamish, The Living Museum of the North, Beamish, County Durham DH9 0RG. Telephone: 0191 370 4000. Website: www.beamish.org.uk

Cotswold Motoring Museum and Toy Collection, The Old Mill, Bourton-on-the-Water, Gloucestershire GL54 2BY. Telephone: 01451 821255. Website: www.cotswold-motoring-museum.co.uk

Lakeland Motor Museum, Old Blue Mill, Backbarrow, Ulverston, Cumbria LA12 3HE. Telephone: 01539 558509. Website: www.lakelandmotormuseum.co.uk

National Motor Museum, John Montagu Building, Beaulieu, Brockenhurst, Hampshire SO42 7ZN. Telephone: 01590 612345. Website: www.beaulieu.co.uk

A fine collection of publicity posters produced by the Shell oil company during the 1930s can be seen at Upton House, near Banbury, Oxfordshire OX15 6HT (telephone: 01295 670266). Upton House is a National Trust property and was the home of Walter Samuel, second Viscount Bearsted, who was chairman of Shell from 1921 to 1946.

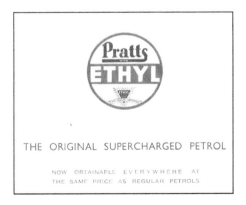

THE ORIGINAL SUPERCHARGED PETROL

NOW OBTAINABLE EVERYWHERE AT
THE SAME PRICE AS REGULAR PETROLS

Pratts referred to its petrol with added ethyl as 'supercharged' petrol. Supercharging of the engine on racing and sports cars was a popular way of gaining extra power, by forcing petrol into the engine from the carburettor under pressure. By using the description 'supercharged', Pratts suggested that its petrol might give the same effect!

Index